Sweet and Easy
Japanese Desserts
Matcha, Mochi and More!

LAURE KIÉ

TUTTLE Publishing

Tokyo | Rutland, Vermont | Singapore

Contents

Why I Wrote This Book

When you think of the iconic dishes that make up Japanese cuisine, a range of tasty savory dishes probably springs to mind. The pastries, confections and sweets that are found in a traditional Western dessert course are far less known. It's true that in Japan, meals don't normally end in dessert. But that doesn't mean the Japanese don't satisfy their sweet cravings at other times and in other ways.

It's not surprising that a cookbook centering on Japanese desserts taps into a long and rich tradition. Many of us are familiar with the sculptural jewels know as wagashi, some so delicately constructed they seem like dainty food souvenirs too precious to eat. That's until you actually take your first bite and realize wagashi are meant to be enjoyed with the eyes before their taste is savored.

Many Japanese pastries and desserts reflect the flora and changing beauty of the seasons, a further testament to the endless adaptability of the nation's cuisine. As with savory dishes, presentation is key, whether it's a fresh-out-of-the-oven confection sprinkled with sesame seeds or a quickbread that's meant to be boxed, wrapped and gifted to a friend.

Like the fare of all nations, Japanese desserts have absorbed a variety of international influences—ranging from French macarons to Portuguese castella, American cheescake, Chinese buns and many more. The fusion of global flavors with traditional Japanese tastes has yielded many sweetly pleasing results!

—Laure Kié

Dozo tameshite
kudasai !

Laure Kié

Born in Tokyo to a Japanese mother and French father, her many trips to Japan helped nuture her passion for Japanese food culture, which she imparts and interprets through her books and cooking classes.

Japanese Desserts

Sweets are the great unknown of Japanese cooking. Traditionally enjoyed at tea time or at special occasions, Japanese sweets and desserts are a must. With the emergence of new tastes, old-school recipes are now being revisited by contemporary chefs and revised to suit contemporary tastes. This mix of originality and tradition is giving rise to a new style of Japanese confection that's varied, subtle, modern and original. Whether enjoyed with a cup of matcha tea or as the final course of a delicious meal, the sweet side of Japanese cuisine offers its own world of surprises and satisfactions.

Ingredients and Utensils

Japanese baking requires only a few key ingredients and implements. You'll find the ingredients at Asian markets, online and at your local supermarket.

The four ingredients you'll need for most of the recipes in this book are: sticky rice flour (needed to make Mochi and Daifuku but also Sweet Coconut Buns; see page 17), red beans or adzuki beans for the Anko-paste-based recipes (see page 24), matcha green tea powder (see page 34) and cornstarch to blend or sprinkle on Mochi (see page 28). Let's take a closer look at these key elements and some other essential ingredients you'll come across in the world of Japanese sweets.

Ingredients

Black sesame paste

Baked adzuki
red beans

Red beans/
adzuki beans

Coconut milk

Yellow mung beans

Matcha green tea powder

Silky tofu

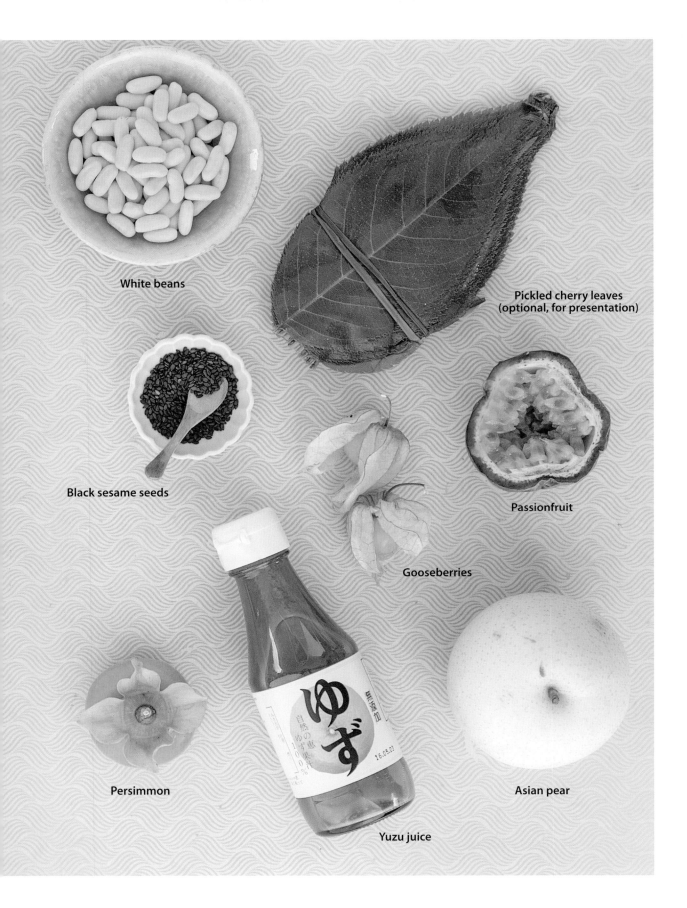

White beans

Pickled cherry leaves
(optional, for presentation)

Black sesame seeds

Passionfruit

Gooseberries

Persimmon

Yuzu juice

Asian pear

Ingredients

What sets Japanese baking apart? Sweet bean pastes and sticky rice are the stars, rather than the wheat flours and dairy products commonly found in Western desserts. Legumes prove a perfect base for layering on both savory and sweet flavors. While a range of beans make an appearance here, it's the adzuki, or red bean, that lies at the heart of most traditional pastries. Fruit, sesame seeds and matcha green tea also contribute their particular profiles. Here's a roundup of some ingredients I've used for the recipes in this book.

Adzuki Red Beans

After soy, this is the most commonly consumed bean in Japan. Appearing in paste form in most desserts (see the Anko Paste recipe on page 24), you can buy them dry or precooked and canned.

Cherry Tree Leaves

These pickled leaves are used as wrappers for Sakura Mochi (see the recipe on page 48), a sweet that's popular during cherry blossom season. You can find them in Japanese grocery stores, Asian markets, online or make them yourself (see the recipe on page 50).

Japanese Fruit

Today, Japanese fruits, such as persimmons and Asian pears, are increasingly available in the West. Yuzu is the new star of the Japanese fruit bowl. You can read more about it on the next page.

Matcha Green Tea Powder

Matcha is a green tea in powder form that is used for the tea ceremony in Japan (see page 34). It has become a must in Japanese baking, so a whole chapter of this book has been devoted to this new favorite flavor (see pages 98–121)!

Sesame Seeds

In Japanese cooking, you'll find both white and black sesame. Whether in the form of seeds or paste, black sesame is preferred in baking for its color and distinctive taste. You can find it in health food stores or Asian grocery stores.

Silky Tofu

Soft, silky soy milk is a great base for puddings and creams. Tofu has spread throughout the world, embraced for its versatility and ability to absorb flavors. Silky tofu is the most common form used in pastries (see the recipe on page 90).

Yellow Mung Beans

Popular in China and Southeast Asia, yellow mung beans are featured here primarily as tasty pastry fillings (see page 132).

Yuzu

This mild citrus fruit commonly used in Japanese sweets is increasingly beloved by Western bakers. Prized for its delicate fragrance and fusion of sour and sweet notes, it's a subtle mix of lemon and clementine. If you can't locate it in its fresh form, you can find bottled juice or the zest in powdered form in Asian grocery shops.

White Beans

Used to make Shiro-an (see page 26), which is one of the bases for Wagashi, there are many varieties of white beans. I recommend using larger ones, since they're easier to prepare. Choose precooked ones if you want to save time when preparing the Shiro-an.

Flours

Standard sticky
rice flour

Tapioca flour

Rice flour

Shiratamako
sticky rice flour

Potato starch

Kuzu flour

Agar-agar
powder or sheets

Tapioca

Kinako toasted
soybean flour

Uncooked sticky rice

Flours & Starches

Agar-Agar Powder or Sheets

Widely used in Japan, this versatile ingredient, a great vegan substitute for traditional animal-based thickeners, comes from seaweed and red algae. See page 32 for a basic recipe.

Kinako Toasted Soybean Flour

Made from roasted soybeans, kinako is often used for desserts in Japan, most notably in Warabi Mochi (see page 68). You can also substitute it for cornstarch for that final sprinkle on Daifuku to give that confection a smoky taste.

Kuzu Root Flour

Kuzu root produces a starch that serves as a thickening agent in sauces. Used in the preparation of Kuzu Manju (see the recipe on page 46), the result is gelatinous while still retaining a creamy texture.

Potato Starch or Cornstarch

Starch is mostly made of glucose, sugar molecules that thicken when added to hot liquid. Potato starch or cornstarch can combined with flour gives dough more elasticity. You can use potato starch and cornstarch interchangeably in these recipes. In Japan, it's mostly used to prevent Mochi dough from sticking (see the recipe on page 28).

Rice Flour

As with wheat flours, rice flour is available ground to varying degrees of fineness. Rice flour is used in the Dango recipe on page 42 and can be substituted for wheat flour for a completely gluten-free version.

Sticky Rice Flour

An essential ingredient for most of the recipes featured here, including the Mochi dough used to make Daifuku (see page 38), sticky rice flour can be found in different forms and under different names. The two most common are: **Shiratamako** (available in Japanese grocery stores) whose fine texture dissolves easily in water for a silky result, and **Mochiko** (or standard sticky rice flour), which typically comes in powdered form and is easier to find in most Asian grocery stores. Both types can be used interchangeably.

Tapioca Flour

Tapioca is a starch derived from the cassava root. The distinctive pearl-like beads are featured in a range of Asian dishes including desserts, breakfasts or sweet drinks. You'll find a tapioca-based recipe on page 124.

Warabiko Starch

Warabiko is a starch made from bracken (an edible fern). It's used for making a dessert with a surprising texture, Warabi Mochi (see the recipe on page 68). Since it's difficult to find, it can be substituted with tapioca flour or sweet potato starch.

Wheat Flour

Whole wheat flour retains more of the bran, resulting in a blend that's richer in nutrients. The whiter the flour appears, the lower the ratio: less bran equals fewer nutrients.

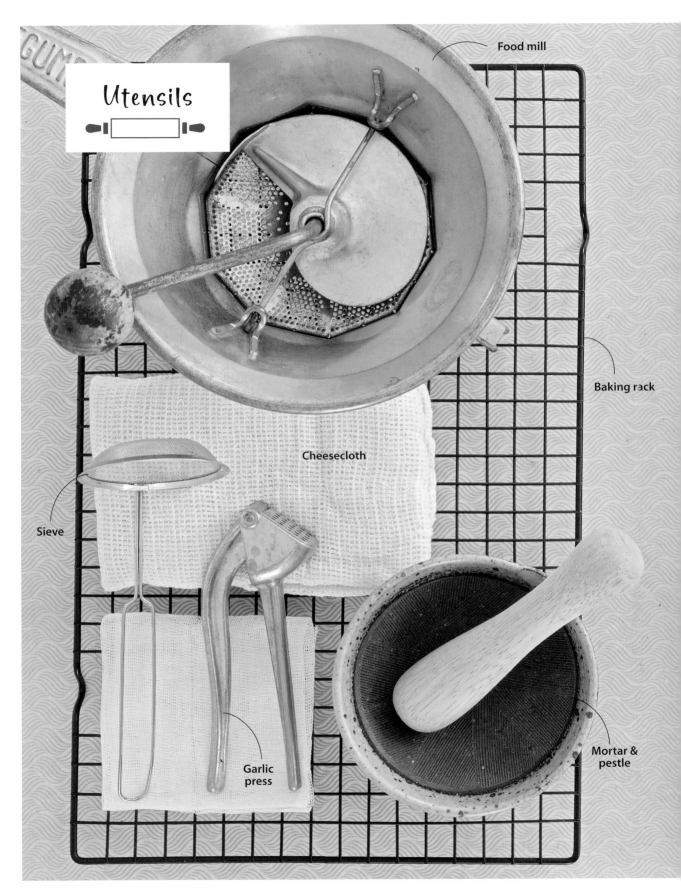

Utensils

Food mill

Baking rack

Cheesecloth

Sieve

Garlic press

Mortar & pestle

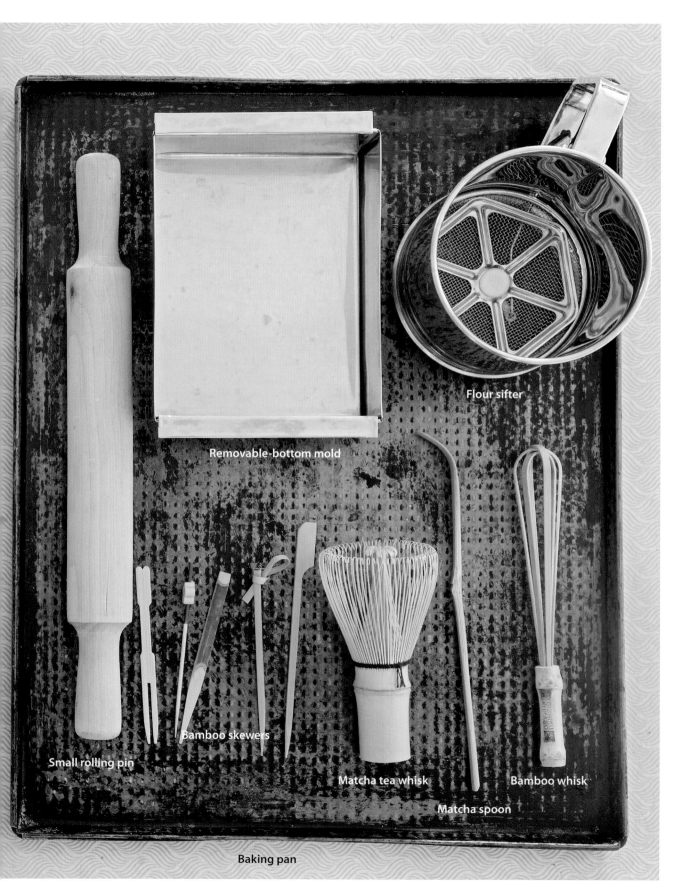

Flour sifter

Removable-bottom mold

Bamboo skewers

Small rolling pin

Matcha tea whisk

Bamboo whisk

Matcha spoon

Baking pan

Wrapping Desserts

In Japan, when it comes to food, presentation is as important as taste. Pastries are usually wrapped in pretty packages that are a visual treat. You can easily make your own one-of-a-kind presents by reusing boxes you have on hand or you can even customize an egg carton. Nothing compares to giving a friend a gift of Wagashi (see page 64) in a charming handmade box!

PREPARATION: 15 minutes
COOKING TIME: 15 minutes

Tools
A small cardboard box
Wrapping or origami paper
String
Scissors
One skewer

1 Gather everything you'll need, while your baked gift is thoroughly cooling.
2 Wrap the box with your paper of choice.
3 Add paper cutouts or other embellishments.
4 Tie the box with string, inserting a skewer underneath and you're done. Watch a smile form on your friend's or loved one's face, then watch your goodies disappear!

Basic Recipes

Before you start baking the Japanese way, let's prepare a few basic recipes that serve as the building blocks for many of the distinctive desserts you'll be making. You'll be turning to the recipes for Mochi dough (that sticky rice paste common in Wagashi) and adzuki-based Anko Paste again and again, so make a big batch and freeze the extra. Then you'll always have some on hand!

Anko Sweet Red Bean Paste

Anko bean paste is used in many Japanese desserts. You can buy it readymade in cans and packets in Asian grocery stores, but you can also prepare your own at home. You just need to plan ahead! There are two types of Anko Paste: Tsubu-an, in which the adzuki beans are only slightly crushed, and Koshi-an, in which the beans are pushed through a sieve or mill to remove the skins and produce a smooth paste. This recipe yields just over 3 cups (1 kg) of Anko Paste, enough to make a number of different desserts. Keep the extra in the freezer until you're ready to use it.

PREPARATION: 20 minutes
COOKING TIME: 2 hours 10 minutes
RESTING TIME: 12 hours

MAKES 2¼ LBS (or a little more than 3 cups/1 kg)

2½ cups (500 g) dry adzuki beans
1¾ cups (360 g) superfine sugar

1 In a pot filled with cold water, soak the beans for at least 12 hours.

2 Drain the beans, then rinse and return them to the pot. Cover with at least twice their volume in water. Place the pot on high heat, bring it to a boil and let the beans cook for 1½ to 2 hours, adding water, if necessary, as needed. When the beans are done, drain them and let them cool slightly.

3 For Koshi-an, turn the beans into a loose paste in a food processor or food mill, then strain it through a fine-mesh sieve. For Tsubu-an, crush the beans slightly with the back of a spoon or a fork.

4 Add the bean paste or crushed beans to a saucepan and, over low heat, add the sugar, stirring until thoroughly incorporated, 2 to 3 minutes.

For Tsubu-an For this chunkier version, leave the cooked beans intact. Use a spoon to crush them or a fork to give them a light mash.

For Koshi-an Turn the beans into a loose paste in a food processor, then strain it through a fine-mesh sieve, discarding the skins.

HINT
To save time, you can put the cooked beans in a blender instead of using a mill; however, the resulting purée won't be as smooth.

Anko Paste Variations

There are many varieties of the Anko Paste that's used in Japanese baking. Shiro-an is made from white beans (shiro means "white"), while Mame-an comes from fava beans, giving you a colorful palette to choose from when creating your Wagashi!

Shiro-an Sweet White Bean Paste

PREPARATION: 20 minutes
COOKING TIME: 2 hours 10 minutes
RESTING TIME: 12 hours

MAKES 2¼ LBS (1 KG) SHIRO-AN

2½ cups (500 g) dry white beans
1¾ cups (360 g) superfine sugar

1 Soak the beans for at least 12 hours in a large pot filled with water.
2 Drain, rinse and then add them to a pan. Cover the beans with at least three times their volume in water, then bring to a boil. Skim the foam and cook for about 2 hours.
3 Drain them, then put them through a food mill or use a food processor. Put the paste in a heavy-bottomed pan and add the sugar.
4 Cook while stirring continuously for 8 to 10 minutes. Let cool.

> **HINT**
> You can prepare Shiro-an starting with a can of pre-cooked white beans. Process 2 cups of cooked beans in a blender, then cook on the stovetop with ¾ cup superfine sugar to make 1⅓ cups of Shiro-an.

Mame-an Sweet Fava Bean Paste

PREPARATION: 15 minutes
COOKING TIME: 15 minutes

MAKES 12 OZ (340 G)

2 cups (250 g) husked frozen or
   fresh fava beans
¾ cup (150 g) superfine sugar

1 Cook the fava beans in boiling water for 15 minutes.
2 Drain then, then put them through a food mill until a smooth paste forms.
3 Spread the paste in a heavy-bottomed pan. Add the sugar. Cook while stirring for 8 to 10 minutes. Let cool.

Shiro-an

Koshi-an

Mame-an

Mochi Sticky Rice Flour Dough

This dough is traditionally made by pounding steamed sticky rice in a mortar (see the recipe on page 48). Here I offer you a quicker recipe using sticky rice flour. This version is used to make a classic treat, Matcha Ice Cream Mochi (check out the recipe on page 80).

PREPARATION: 15 minutes
COOKING TIME: 15 minutes

MAKES 1¼ LBS (575 G)

1¼ cups (200 g) sticky rice flour
1¼ cups (300 ml) water
⅓ cup (75 g) superfine sugar
Potato or cornstarch, for dusting

HINT
You can use different sticky rice flours for this recipe, such as shiratamoko or joshinko. See page 16 for more info.

1 In a bowl, mix the sticky rice flour, water and sugar.
2 Prepare the water in a steamer. Set the bowl in the steamer's tray, then cover and steam for 15 minutes.
3 Sift some starch onto a work surface and turn the cooked dough out onto the surface using a spatula.
4 Sprinkle more starch liberally over the surface as the dough will be very sticky. Wrap it tightly then chill it until you're ready to use it.

Instead of steaming it, you can cook the Mochi in a microwave oven for 1–2 minutes at a time. Check the dough, then cook it for another 1–2 minutes until it's semi-transparent. It's very easy to overcook it, so do it in stages and keep a watchful eye on the progress.

Nerikiri Dough

Nerikiri is a dough made by combining Shiro-an Sweet White Bean Paste (see page 26) and sticky rice flour. It's the base for confections such as Wagashi (see pages 64–67 for the recipes). Food coloring is added to the dough to create the stunning visual variety these traditional desserts are known for.

PREPARATION: 15 minutes
COOKING TIME: 20 minutes
RESTING TIME: 30 minutes

MAKES 1¼ LBS (575 G)

1½ cups (500 g) Shiro-an Sweet White Bean Paste (see page 26)
2 tablespoons (25 g) sticky rice flour
A few drops food coloring (green, yellow and pink)

1 Mix the Shiro-an and the sticky rice flour to create a dough. Boil some water and set the dough over it in a steamer basket and wrapped in cheesecloth for 20 minutes.

2 Move the dough to a work surface and knead it with the cloth until it's smooth. Let it cool for 30 minutes, then divide the dough into three equal portions.

3 Set one portion in a bowl. Sprinkle a few drops of green food coloring on top, mixing it until the dough is smooth and the color is consistent. Repeat for the yellow and pink Nerikiri, using the respective food colorings.

4 Use your tricolored balls of Nerikiri for making traditional and elegantly sculpted Wagashi.

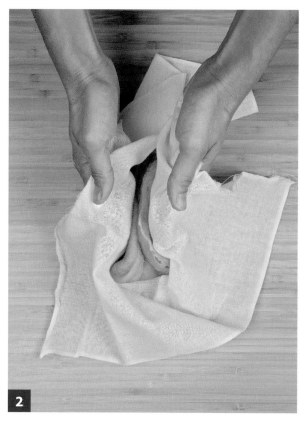

Using Agar-Agar

This natural thickener is made from seaweed. While in the West, animal-based gelatin is common, agar-agar is the thickener most widely used in Japan. You can find it sold in filament form and in sheets, but I suggest you buy the powdered version, which is much easier to use, especially when making Agar-Agar Fruit Jelly (see the recipe on page 58).

PREPARATION: 5 minutes
COOKING TIME: 5 minutes
RESTING TIME: 15 minutes

MAKES 2 CUPS (500 G)

4¼ cups (1 l) cold water
5 teaspoons (10 g) agar-agar powder

1 Amount: The difficulty with agar-agar is in using the correct amount since it's more concentrated than gelatin. To thicken a cup of water, add 1 teaspoon (2g) of powdered agar-agar. If you want a thicker, more solid consistency, use slightly more than 1 teaspoon.

2 Cooking: Agar-agar needs to be incorporated into a cold liquid. Whisk it into the water in a saucepan while the water is still room temperature. Then place it on the stove. As soon as it comes to a boil, turn the heat to low and simmer for another 5 minutes.

3 Gelification: Thickening and solidifaction will occur when the preparation cools to around 105°F (40°C). Pour the liquid into a container and let it chill in the fridge until it's ready. It should be set after an hour or two.

Matcha Green Tea

There are many green tea varieties: sencha (the most popular), bancha (often the cheapest), hojicha (roasted), genmaicha (tea with toasted rice grains), gyokuro (tea from young seedlings) and, finally, matcha green tea powder. Matcha is the type used as the centerpiece of the traditional tea ceremony.

PREPARATION: 15 minutes
COOKING TIME: 20 minutes
RESTING TIME: 30 minutes

Matcha Ingredients
Water at 175°F (80°C)
1 teaspoon matcha powder

Utensils Needed
A bowl
Chasen (bamboo whisk)
**Chashaku (bamboo spoon,
 optional)**

1 Start by pouring hot water in the bowl to heat it. After a minute or so, drain the water and return the bowl to the table.
2 Add the matcha powder to the bowl.
3 Pour about 3 tablespoons of hot water (about 175° F) onto the powder.
4 Using the whisk, dilute the powder, whisking it on the surface of the water to form the letter M and making sure the whisk doesn't touch the bottom of the bowl. When foam forms on the top, slow down and remove the whisk delicately without disturbing the foam.

This beverage, with its subtle bitterness, is enjoyed on its own at teatime or often accompanied by a sweet.

Traditional Wagashi Pastries

Traditional Japanese pastries are called Wagashi ("wa" here means Japanese and "kashi" translates to sweets). These tiny confections are enjoyed first for their presentation, then for their refined and delicate taste. Often resembling gems, they're meant to evoke elements of the natural world. The best examples are made for cherry blossom season, when the confections conjure those elegant and ephemeral flowers. Wagashi are enjoyed with green tea during the iconic tea ceremony, when matcha is always served with one of these sculptural treats.

Daifuku Red Bean Mochi

Consisting of a layer of Mochi sticky rice dough stuffed with Anko Sweet Red Bean Paste, Daifuku is one of the most common and beloved Japanese confections. The best part is they're supereasy to make at home. Once you get the hang of it, you'll be making these tasty treats all the time!

PREPARATION: 15 minutes
COOKING TIME: 20 minutes
RESTING TIME: 30 minutes

MAKES 8

⅘ cup (200 g) Koshi-an Anko Sweet Red Bean Paste (see page 24)
¾ cup (100 g) sticky rice flour
¼ cup (50 g) superfine sugar
⅔ cup (150 ml) water
Potato starch or cornstarch, for dusting

1 Divide the Koshi-an into 8 parts, then form it into 8 balls. Put them in the fridge while you prepare the mochi dough wrappers.
2 In a bowl, mix the sticky rice flour, sugar and water. Let the mixture stand while you prepare a steamer.
3 Set the bowl with the dough in the steamer, cover it and steam the contents for 15 minutes.
4 Sprinkle starch on a work surface and turn the cooked dough onto it using a spatula. Apply starch liberally to the dough as it'll be very sticky and then flatten it out with your fingers.
5 Spread or flatten out the dough using your hands or a floured rolling pin.
6 Cut the dough into 8 equal parts.
7 Take one portion of the dough and flatten it in the palm of your hand. Set an Anko ball on top of the dough then wrap it with the dough, entirely enclosing it.
8 Repeat for the seven remaining Daifuku. Serve on individual plates with small forks.

Matcha variation: Mix 1 tablespoon of matcha powder with the sticky rice flour before steaming the dough.

Kinako variation: Substitute kinako for the starch used for dusting the Mochi dough, to give it a brown coating and a smoky flavor.

Fruit variation: See the recipe on page 76.

How to Make Daifuku

1

4

5

6

Dango Mochi Balls

Dango is a slightly sweet Mochi dumpling made from a mixture of rice flours. Chewy and tender yet still firm, they're perfect for a Japanese-inspired high tea. But most folks know them from their common street-snack format: skewered on a stick as shown.

PREPARATION: 15 minutes
COOKING TIME: 6 minutes

MAKES 15 BALLS or 5 SKEWERS

¼ cup (50 g) rice flour
Scant 1 cup (110 g) sticky rice flour
3 heaping tablespoons (50 g)
   superfine sugar
1 tablespoon matcha powder
6 tablespoons (90 ml) hot water
A few drops red food coloring

HINT
If you wish, you can use all sticky rice flour instead of the rice flour-sticky rice flour mix.

1 Mix the flours and sugar in a bowl. Divide the mixture evenly among three bowls.
2 Mix the matcha with 2 tablespoons of hot water and add it to the first bowl. Mix until the dough is soft. Adjust the water or flour quantity in order to achieve the proper balance. Then form five balls.
3 Add the red food coloring to 2 tablespoons of hot water in the second bowl. Pour the last 2 tablespoons of hot water into the last bowl. Form 10 balls from the last two bowls, five green ones and five white.
4 Bring water to a boil in a large pan. Add the balls in batches. Once they float, let them cook for 2 extra minutes, then drain and remove them. Place a ball of each color on a skewer and enjoy.

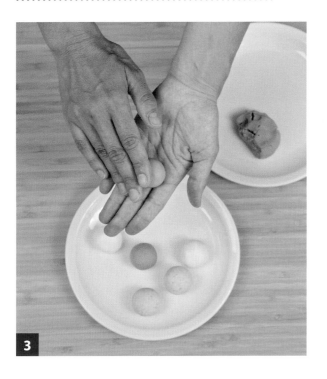

Dorayaki Red Bean Pancakes

Take two fluffy pancakes made of castella batter, slather sweet adzuki bean paste in between and you've just made Dorayaki, an elegant sandwich-style confection. If you want to transform these treats, use matcha cream, chocolate-hazelnut spread or custard cream instead of the red bean paste for a flavorful filling that's a departure from the ordinary.

PREPARATION: 10 minutes
COOKING TIME: 20 minutes

MAKES ABOUT 6 PANCAKES

2 eggs
⅓ cup (70 g) superfine sugar
1 tablespoon honey
A pinch of salt
1 tablespoon baking powder
1 tablespoon water
1 heaping cup (140 g) flour
1 teaspoon vegetable oil
1 cup (320 g) Tsubu-an Anko Sweet
   Red Bean Paste (see the recipe on
   page 24)

1 Mix the eggs, sugar, honey and salt in a bowl. Whisk for about 2 minutes. Dilute the baking powder in the water, then whisk it into the mixture. Sift the flour, add it to the bowl and mix.

2 Heat the oil in a nonstick pan on medium.

3 Pour about 2 tablespoons of batter into the pan. Lightly spread it out to create a small circle. As soon as small bubbles form on the surface, flip the pancake. Cook the other side until it's golden, then set it aside.

4 To assemble, spread a small amount of Tsubu-an on a pancake, then top it with a second pancake. Press the two halves gently together. Repeat the process to create at least six Dorayaki.

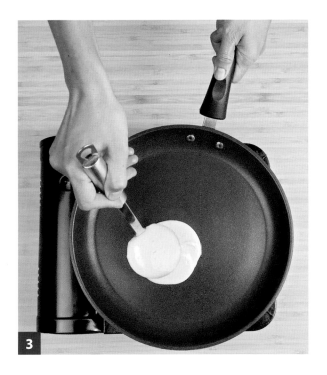

Fava Bean Kuzu Manju

A summertime treat since the Edo period, kuzu manju is a study in contrasts. While the exterior can be gelatinous and a little chewy, the filling is the sweetly smooth reward. Here a fava bean paste is used as the filling instead of the traditional Anko. For an extra-special presentation, serve the Manju on bamboo leaves or wrap them up to form cones.

PREPARATION: 20 minutes
COOKING TIME: 5 minutes

MAKES ABOUT 10

6 heaping tablespoons (50 g) kuzu starch (found in health food stores and Asian grocery stores)
¾ cup plus 1 tablespoon (200 ml) water
6 tablespoons (80 g) superfine sugar
1 portion Mame-an Sweet Fava Bean Paste (see page 26)
Fresh or frozen bamboo leaves for wrapping (optional, available at Asian markets or online)

1 Prepare the Mame-an Sweet Fava Bean Paste by following the recipe on page 26. Form the paste into 10 small balls then set them in the fridge to chill.
2 Mix the kuzu and water in a saucepan until the kuzu dissolves. Blend in the sugar. Cook the mixture on low heat, using a spatula until it becomes a translucent paste. Remove a tablespoon of the paste and drop it into a bowl of cold water. Remove it, drain it on a towel, then flatten it into a small disk in your palm. Place a small ball of the Sweet Fava Bean Paste in the center, enclosing the stuffing with the kuzu dough.
3 Repeat for the remaining 9 manju. Let them cool before serving.

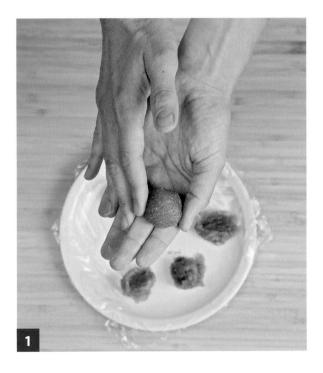

Sakura "Cherry Blossom" Mochi

Sweet pink Mochi is wrapped in a preserved cherry leaf for a one-of-a-kind treat. Remember that the leaves are for presentation purposes only. Remove them before eating!

PREPARATION: 15 minutes
COOKING TIME: 15 minutes
RESTING TIME: 1 hour 30 minutes

MAKES ABOUT 10

1¼ cups (250 g) uncooked sticky rice
2 tablespoons superfine sugar
2 drops red coloring
1½ cups water
¾ cup (250 g) Koshi-an Anko Sweet Red Bean Paste (see the recipe on page 24)
10 Pickled Cherry Tree Leaves (see the recipe on the next page, or buy them at a Japanese market or online)

HINT
If you can't find Pickled Cherry Tree Leaves, add a pinch of salt to the cooking water in Step 1 so you'll get the salty taste characteristic of this recipe.

1 Rinse the rice several times. Drain it, then add it to a saucepan with the sugar, food coloring and water. Let the rice soak for an hour.

2 Cover the pan, bring it to a boil, then lower the heat and cook the mixture for 12 minutes. Remove it from the heat and let it stand for 15 minutes uncovered, then mix well with a spoon.

3 In the meantime, form the Koshi-an Red Bean Paste into 10 small balls. Chill them in the fridge.

4 Soak the cherry tree leaves in a bowl of water for 15 minutes. Drain, then dry the leaves with a paper towel.

5 Put the cooked rice in a large mortar and pound it until a rough paste forms.

6 Place 1 heaping tablespoon of the rice paste on a work surface or a piece of plastic wrap. Wet your fingers and flatten the rice paste lightly to form a disk. Put a small Koshi-an ball in the center.

7 Enclose it with the rice paste. You can use plastic wrap if you find the dough too sticky.

8 Remove the plastic wrap and enclose the mochi in a pickled cherry tree leaf folded in half.

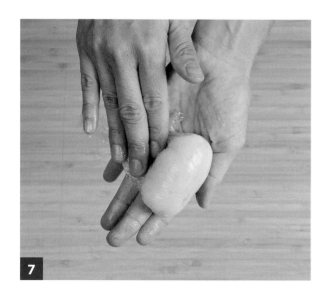

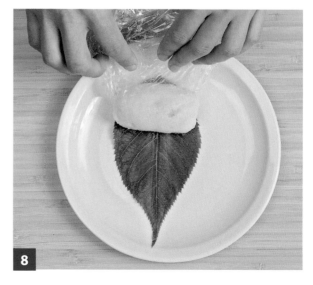

Pickled Cherry Tree Leaves

MAKES 20 LEAVES

1 teaspoon salt
2 tablespoons hot water
20 young cherry tree leaves
  (harvested in spring)

1 In a bowl, dissolve the salt in the water, then cool it to room temperature.

2 Fill a large pot with water and bring it to a boil. Blanch the leaves for 1 minute. Drain them, then shock them in an ice water bath. Drain the leaves, then add them to a plastic bag containing the cooled salted water. Pickle in the fridge for at least 2 days.

3 When the desired time has expired, drain the leaves. They'll keep for one month in the fridge or for a year in the freezer. You can also buy pickled, salted sakura leaves ready to use in Japanese and Asian grocery stores and online.

Mizu Yokan Bars

This yokan, or chilled red bean jelly, uses "mizu"—the Japanese word for water—to achieve its delicacy of flavor. Perfect with a cup of matcha, the slightly sweet Anko bean flavor complements the earthiness of the green tea.

PREPARATION: 5 minutes
COOKING TIME: 3 minutes
RESTING TIME: 2 hours

SERVES 8 TO 10

⅔ cup (150 ml) water
A pinch salt
1½ teaspoons (3 g) agar-agar powder
1⅓ cups (400 g) Anko Sweet Red Bean Paste (Koshi-an, see page 24)

1 Mix the water, salt, anko and agar-agar in a saucepan.
2 Bring it to a boil and cook for 30 seconds while stirring constantly with a whisk.
3 Pour the preparation into a small cake pan with a removable bottom (or use a springform pan or a regular cake pan lined with plastic wrap). Let it cool until it reaches room temperature, then place it in the fridge for at least 2 hours.
4 Unmold the mizu yokan and cut it into small slices before serving.

HINT
You can elevate this sweet, enjoyed in Japan with green tea, by adding nuts to the cake mold before pouring in the Anko. Chestnuts in a light syrup make for a nice finishing touch too.

Anpan Red Bean Buns

This ultimate Japanese sweet roll conceals a tasty dollop of creamy Anko Sweet Red Bean Paste inside. Other fillings are also used—white beans, chestnuts and sesame—but sometimes nothing beats the original. Poppy seeds are the traditional topping, but black sesame seeds make a gorgeous garnish too.

PREPARATION: 30 minutes
COOKING TIME: 12 minutes
RESTING TIME: 1 hour 55 minutes

MAKES 10

¼ cup (50 g) superfine sugar
1½ tablespoons baking powder
⅓ cup plus 1 tablespoon (100 ml) milk
1 cup (320 g) Anko Sweet Red Bean Paste (Tsubu-an, see the recipe on page 24)
2 cups (250 g) flour
1 tablespoon cornstarch
A pinch of salt
1 egg, beaten
2½ tablespoons (35 g) unsalted butter, at room temperature

For the Garnish
1 egg
Black sesame seeds, to taste
A pinch of salt

1 Dilute the sugar and the baking powder with the milk in a bowl and let it sit for 5 minutes.

2 In a mixing bowl, combine the flour, cornstarch and salt. Add the sugar mixture and blend. Then add the beaten egg, stirring again. Cut the butter into small cubes, then add it to the dough.

3 Knead the dough for about 10 minutes. If necessary, adjust the consistency by adding milk if the dough is too dry or flour if it's too sticky. Form it into a ball, then place it in a mixing bowl.

4 Cover the dough with a towel and let it rest in a warm place for about an hour; the dough has to rise and double in volume.

5 When the dough has doubled, kneed it quickly to remove excess air. Divide it into 8 equal portions. Set them on a baking sheet lined with parchment paper. Cover the baking sheet with plastic wrap and let it stand for 15 minutes.

6 In the meantime, form 8 small balls of Anko using an ice cream scoop.

Anpan Red Bean Buns (continued)

7 Sprinkle flour onto a work surface. Take a dough ball, spread it out to get a 4-inch (10-cm) circle. Add a small ball of the Anko Red Bean Paste.

8 Enclose it with the dough, then let the ball rest 30 minutes on the baking sheet under plastic wrap.

9 Preheat the oven to 395°F (200°C).

10 In a bowl, beat the egg with a pinch of salt and water. Brush the dough balls with the beaten egg. Sprinkle them with the sesame seeds.

11 Bake for 12 minutes. Cool slightly before serving.

To store the anpan and keep them soft, wrap them in a towel and keep them in an airtight container.

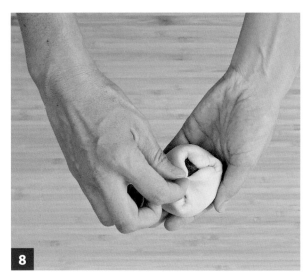

Agar-Agar Fruit Jelly

This light summery finale offers impromptu opportunities for presentation and serving. While small dessert bowls are ideal, use whatever's on hand: juice glasses, paper cups, ice cube trays, muffin tins. It'll taste great no matter what form it comes in! For instructions on how to prepare the agar-agar, refer to pages 32–33.

PREPARATION: 30 minutes
COOKING TIME: 3 minutes
RESTING TIME: 2 hours 30 minutes

SERVES 6

2 kiwi fruit
1 cup (160 g) cape gooseberries or kumquats
2 cups (475 ml) water
2 teaspoons (4 g) agar-agar powder
½ cup (100g) superfine sugar
2 tablespoons yuzu juice (or a mix of orange and lemon juice)

1 Peel then dice the kiwis and the gooseberries.
2 In a saucepan, mix the water, agar-agar and sugar. Bring it to a boil, while stirring constantly. Remove from the heat as soon as the sugar is dissolved. Divide the mixture evenly among six ramekins (or whatever container you're using) and let them sit for 5 minutes.
3 Divide the kiwis and gooseberry dice among the six ramekins or containers. Then divide the yuzu juice evenly on top of the six jellies as well.
4 Let them cool to room temperature and chill in the fridge for at least 2 hours before serving.

HINT
This recipe can be prepared the day before or even 2 days in advance. You can of course vary the fruit according to the season.

Manju Steamed Red Bean Buns

Originally a Chinese confection, manju migrated to Japan long ago where it's been an enduringly popular sweet. These easy-to-make dumplings are gently steamed, the sugary carbs and the Anko forming a perfect pair.

PREPARATION: 20 minutes
COOKING TIME: 10 minutes

MAKES ABOUT 12

¾ cup (250 g) **Koshi-an Anko Sweet Red Bean Paste (see page 24)**
1 cup (120 g) **self-rising white flour**
½ cup (80 g) **superfine sugar**
3 tablespoons **water**

1 Divide the Koshi-an into 12 small balls, then set them in the fridge to chill.

2 In a mixing bowl, dissolve the sugar in the water. Sift the flour, then incorporate it, mixing well to obtain an even consistency. Divide the dough into 12 portions. Press and spread out each portion in your palm to form a small disk.

3 Set a Koshi-an ball in the center of each disk, wrapping the dough completely around it. Place it in a steamer lined with a thin cloth or with parchment paper, then repeat with the remaining ingredients.

4 Steam the manju for 10 minutes. Enjoy either hot or at room temperature.

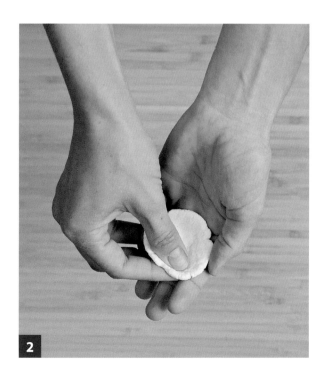

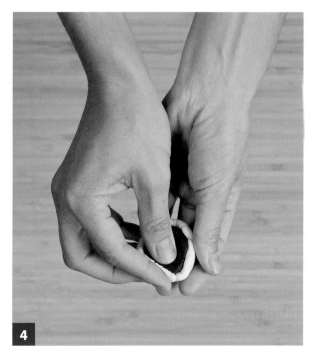

Castella Cake

This moist sponge cake was originally made in wooden frames to create the dark brown crusts and delicate, springy texture. But a loaf pan suffices for this four-ingredient delight!

PREPARATION: 15 minutes
COOKING TIME: 15 minutes
RESTING TIME: 4 hours

SERVES 4

3½ tablespoons (75 g) honey diluted with 3 tablespoons hot water
1 cup (130 g) flour
6 eggs
⅔ cup (120 g) superfine sugar

HINT
Castella keeps well in the fridge for a few days. Make sure to protect it in plastic wrap so it doesn't dry out.

1 Preheat the oven to 360°F (180°C). Reserve 2 tablespoons of the honey mixture. Line an 8-inch (20-cm) long rectangular cakepan with parchment paper. Sift the flour into a mixing bowl.

2 Break the eggs into the bowl of a mixer. Combine them with the sugar, mixing at maximum speed for 5 minutes. Add the honey and mix some more, then add half of the sifted flour. Mix, then add the rest of the flour, mixing one last time. Pour the batter into the prepared pan and bake for 35 minutes.

3 Remove the cake from the oven, then slather it with the reserved honey mixture.

4 Remove the paper and let it cool for at least 4 hours. Cut off the edges of the cake and then slice before serving.

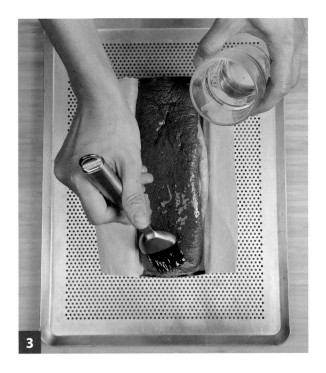

Assorted Wagashi

Wagashi are the art stars of the Japanese dessert course, prompting people to sometimes say, they're just too beautiful to eat! Aki, hana and shibori are three popular wagashi styles and an easy introduction to making these elegant confections at home.

PREPARATION: 45 minutes

MAKES 12 WAGASHI

For the Shibori Wagashi (green and yellow flowers)
3 tablespoons (60 g) Shiro-an Sweet White Bean Paste (see page 26)
2 heaping tablespoons (45 g) green Nerikiri Dough (recipe on page 30)
2 heaping tablespoons (45 g) yellow Nerikiri Dough
1 teaspoon (6 g) yellow Nerikiri Dough (see page 30)

For the Hana Wagashi (pink cherry blossom flowers)
3 tablespoons (60 g) Shiro-an Sweet White Bean Paste (see page 26)
¼ cup (90 g) pink Nerikiri Dough (see page 30)
1 teaspoon (6 g) yellow Nerikiri Dough (see page 30)

Shibori Wagashi (green and yellow):
1 Start by making the Nerikiri Dough on page 30. Form the Shiro-an into three small balls. Divide the green Nerikiri into three small balls, then do the same with the yellow Nerikiri.
2 Lightly flatten one green and one yellow ball between your fingers. Spread out the dough to create a half-green, half-yellow disk. Place the dough on a clean towel.
3 Set a ball of Shiro-an Sweet White Bean Paste in the center and close the towel around the dough.
4 Twist it to form a tight ball. Remove the Wagashi, set aside, then repeat to create the other two.

Hana Wagashi (pink flower):
5 Form the Shiro-an into three balls, then do the same with the pink Nerikiri. Spread out a ball of pink dough in your palm. Set a Shiro-an ball in the center and encase it within the pink dough, forming a ball.
6 Using the dull side of a knife or a toothpick, make eight indentations around the ball to form petals. Set it on a serving dish. Using the round end of a chopstick, press lightly into the center, where the eight lines meet, to form a small indentation.
7 Push the yellow Nerikiri through a fine-mesh sieve using the back of a spoon. Using chopsticks, take some of the thin ribbons and set them delicately on top of the flower. Repeat for the other Wagashi.

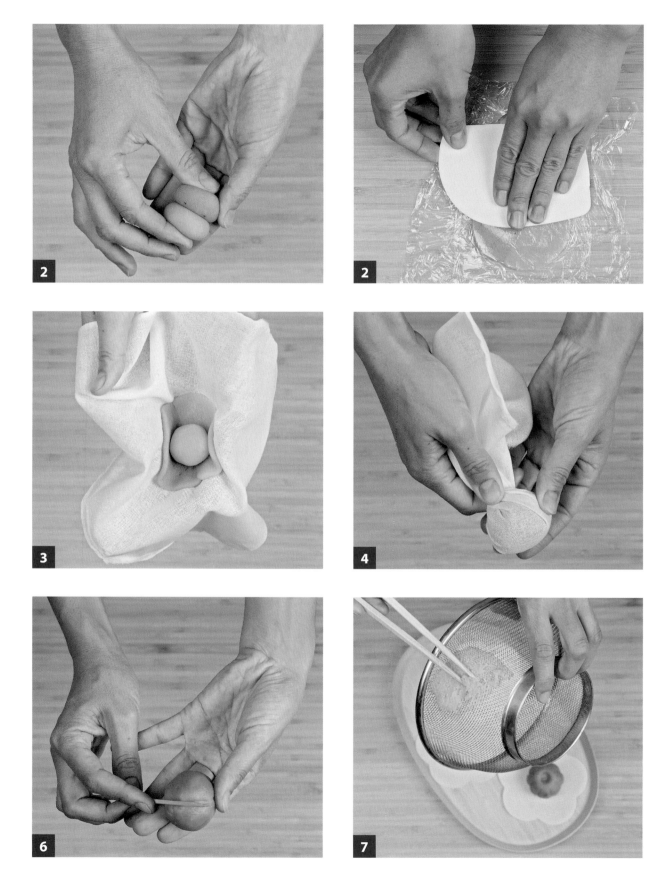

Assorted Wagashi (continued)

For Aki Wagashi (Autumn)
3 tablespoons (60 g) Tsubu-an Anko Sweet Red Bean Paste (see page 24)
2 heaping tablespoons (45 g) green Nerikiri (see page 30)

Aki Wagashi (Autumn)

8 Form the Red Bean Paste into three small balls. Separately push the green and yellow nerikiri through a garlic press or a fine-mesh sieve to create ribbons of dough.

9 Delicately place these ribbons around the Anko balls using chopsticks. Let the paste show through on the top. Repeat for the remaining two Wagashi.

You can of course create other colors, forms and combinations. Let your imagination guide you!

Aki Wagashi

Shibori Wagashi

Hana Wagashi

Warabi Mochi

These chilled, chewy, jelly-like Mochi are traditionally covered in kinako roasted soybean powder and drizzled with molasses-like kuromitsu brown sugar syrup. Here I've made a few adjustments while preserving the flavor of this distinctive dessert. Maple or agave syrups make very good substitutions.

PREPARATION: 10 minutes
COOKING TIME: 5 minutes

SERVES 6

For the Dough
½ cup (60 g) warabiko starch
1¼ cups (300 ml) water
¼ cup (50 g) superfine sugar

For the Garnish
¼ cup (30 g) kinako roasted soybean flour
Agave or maple syrup, to drizzle on top

1 Mix all the ingredients for the dough in a saucepan. Heat on low, whisking all the while until the mixture becomes thick and transparent.
2 Sift half of the kinako onto a baking sheet. Set the cooked dough on top, then sift the rest of the kinako on top.
3 Cut the dough into cubes. Be sure each one is covered in kinako.
4 Pour a little syrup on top and serve.

In place of the warabiko starch, you can substitute ¼ cup (30 g) sticky rice flour and ¼ cup (30 g) tapioca flour, as they're easier to find in Asian and specialty grocery stores.

Modern Desserts

Now that we've had a crash course in the traditional tastes of Wagashi and other old-school desserts, let's explore the Western influences that have infused Japanese baking in recent years. In each case, you will find that Japanese cooks have added their own twists to the Western-style recipes.

Modern confections are showcased here, typified by Japanese cheesecake, which is lighter and less sweet than the American version. It takes its iconic place among Mochi ice cream balls, fruit fried tempura-style and éclairs infused with black sesame!

Melon Pan Sweet Buns

Kashi pan, Japanese sweet buns, have their ardent fans around the world. This crispy-crusted treat with the distinctive lattice-patterned top (a little like grandma's peanut butter cookies) brings a cookie-like quality to the soft satisfying textures of the pastry.

PREPARATION: 1 hour
COOKING TIME: 15 minutes
RESTING TIME: 3 hours

MAKES 6

For the Bread Dough
1 heaping cup (140 g) white flour, plus more for kneading
2 tablespoons superfine sugar
A pinch salt
1 teaspoon (3 g) dry yeast
Scant ⅓ cup (70 ml) milk
1 tablespoon beaten egg
1 tablespoon (15 g) butter, at room temperature

For the Shortbread
4 tablespoons (60 g) butter, at room temperature
¼ cup (50 g) superfine sugar
1 egg, beaten
½ teaspoon baking powder
½ cup (60 g) warabiko or tapioca flour

Preparing the Bread Dough
1 In a bowl, mix the flour, sugar, salt and yeast. In a small saucepan, heat the milk until it's lukewarm. Remove it from heat and add the beaten egg. Add it to the dry ingredients, little by little, while stirring constantly with a spatula. Then place the dough on a floured surface.

2 Knead the dough for 5 minutes, then flatten it into a disk.

3 Dice the butter and place the pieces on top of the dough. Incorporate the butter, kneading for 10 minutes. Form the dough into a ball, then place it in a mixing bowl. Cover it with a towel and let it rise for at least an hour at room temperature.

Preparing the Shortbread
4 In the meanwhile, prepare the shortbread. In a bowl, beat the butter until it's creamy. Add the sugar, little by little, mixing until it's completely dissolved in the butter.

5 Add half of the beaten egg. Mix well, then incorporate the other half. Sift the flour together with the baking powder. Add them, little by little, using a spatula until the dough is smooth. Form the dough into a cylinder, wrap it in plastic and let it chill for an hour in the fridge.

Melon Pan Sweet Buns (continued)

Form the Bread Dough Balls

6 Press a finger into the center of the dough. If the hole doesn't close up, it's ready to transfer to a work surface. It should have roughly doubled in size. Knead it again for 2 minutes in order to remove any excess air.

7 Divide the dough in six equal balls. Set them on a baking sheet covered with plastic wrap, and let them rest for 15 minutes.

Prepare the Shortbread Circles

8 Remove the shortbread dough from the fridge and remove the plastic wrap. Cut it into six equal parts, spreading each into a 5-in (12-cm) disk.

> **HINT**
> To check that the bread dough has risen enough, insert your finger into the middle of the ball (see the photo). If the hole doesn't close, the dough is ready.

Finish the Melon Pan Sweet Buns

9 Preheat the oven to 355°F (180°C).

10 Flatten the bread dough balls on the work surface with the palm of your hand. Use a piece of plastic wrap, if you wish, to prevent sticking.

11 Form each into a ball and cover it with a shortbread circle so that a small part shows at the base (see the photo).

12 Put some sugar in a bowl. Gently press the top of each melon pan sweet bun into the sugar so that the whole surface is covered.

13 With a pastry cutter or knife, make a lattice pattern on top of each.

14 Set them on a baking sheet. Let them rest for 45 minutes.

15 Bake the melon pan sweet bun for 15 minutes, then remove to a baking rack to cool.

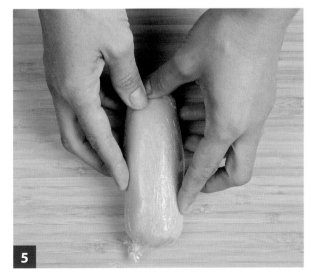

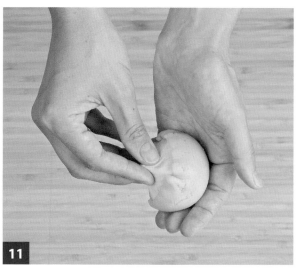

Strawberry Daifuku Mochi

A springtime staple, these soft and chewy rice mochi hold a hidden treat: plump and juicy strawberries. With a little Anko paste to hold it in place, these tiny confections can easily be mistaken for dessert-course works of art.

PREPARATION: 20 minutes
COOKING TIME: 15 minutes

MAKES 8

8 strawberries
4 tablespoons (80 g) Shiro-an
   Sweet White Bean Paste

For the Mochi Dough
⅘ cup (100 g) sticky rice flour
4 tablespoons (50 g) superfine
   sugar
Potato or cornstarch, for dusting

1 Hull the strawberries and set aside. Divide the Shiro-an Sweet Bean Paste into eight small balls.

2 Flatten each ball in your hand, place a strawberry in the center and wrap it with the Shiro-an. Repeat with the rest, then chill them in the fridge.

3 Prepare the Mochi Dough according to the instructions on page 28.

4 Form the Strawberry Daifuku Mochi following the same instructions for plain Daifuku Mochi (see page 38), replacing the Anko balls with strawberries covered in Shiro-an.

HINT
You can make Daifuku using different fruits depending on the season—kiwi, melon, mango, persimmon—whatever catches your eye and strikes your fancy!

2

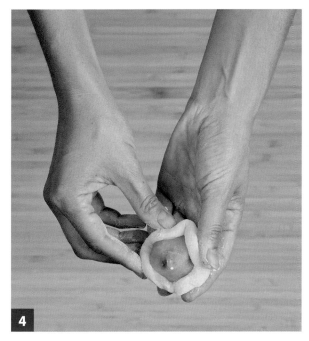

4

Matcha Ice Cream Mochi

The ice cream sandwich has been transformed into a freezer treat that's now very familiar to non-Japanese dessert lovers. Who knew it's just as easy to make your own version at home? Try it with a range of ice cream flavors—tangy apricot, sweet strawberry or other fruity flavors.

PREPARATION: 10 minutes
COOKING TIME: 5 minutes
CHURNING TIME: 25 minutes

**MAKES 4¼ CUPS (900 G) ICE
  CREAM**

3 egg yolks
Scant ½ cup (90 g) superfine sugar
1¼ cups (300 ml) whole milk
1¼ cups (300 ml) whipping cream
2 tablespoons matcha powder

Prepare the Matcha Ice Cream

1 In a mixing bowl, quickly whisk the egg yolks and the sugar until the mixture is foamy.

2 In a saucepan, heat the milk and cream. As soon as it comes to a boil, remove from the heat and incorporate the matcha powder.

3 Pour the still-hot mixture into the sugar-egg mixture, whisking quickly until it's smooth.

4 Return it to a pan on low heat and stir continuously with a spatula as the cream thickens.

5 As soon as the mixture coats the spatula or the back of a spoon, remove it from heat.

6 Let the mixture cool to room temperature, then pour it into an ice cream maker. Churn in the ice cream maker for 25 minutes.

Matcha Ice Cream Mochi (continued)

PREPARATION: 25 minutes
COOKING TIME: 15 minutes

MAKES 15 MOCHI BALLS

1 lb (500 g) warm mochi (see
    page 28)
2 tablespoons potato or cornstarch
2½ cups (600 ml) matcha ice cream

Prepare the Ice Cream Mochi Balls:

7 Set the still-warm Mochi on a work surface dusted with starch.

8 Sprinkle more starch as needed onto the Mochi, to prevent it from sticking, then spread it out to a thickness of ¼ inch (5 mm). Cut 15 circles that are 4 inches (10 cm) in diameter, using a cookie or biscuit cutter or a drinking glass.

9 Stack the circles with layers of plastic wrap between each one, then set them in the freezer for at least 10 minutes to chill.

10 Remove the Mochi circles from the freezer. Set a small scoop of ice cream in the middle of each.

11 Wrap the Mochi around the ice cream using plastic wrap to aid you, if you wish.

12 Enjoy right away or keep them in the freezer for later. Remove a few minutes before serving, to allow the Mochi to soften.

Chocolate Fruit Tempura

This is one of my favorite desserts! Freshly fried fruit tempura slathered in a luscious chocolate sauce isn't an everyday indulgence. If you can't find a persimmon, other fruits are equally delicious: apple, banana, strawberry or pineapple. Or why not try them all?

PREPARATION: 20 minutes
COOKING TIME: 10 minutes

SERVES 4

1 pear (4 oz/120 g)
1 persimmon (5 oz/140 g)
2 oz (2 squares/60 g) dark baking
   chocolate
⅘ cup (100 g) tempura flour
¾ cup plus 1 tablespoon (200 ml)
   chilled water
Oil, for frying

1 Peel and core the pear, then cut it into eight equal portions.

2 Peel the persimmon and cut it into half-moons.

3 Prepare a chocolate coulis by melting the squares in a double-boiler. Leave the chocolate in the boiler until ready to serve.

4 Prepare the tempura batter in a mixing bowl by combining the flour and cold water.

5 Heat the oil to 340°F (170°C).

6 Dip the fruit pieces, a few at a time, into the batter then immediately drop them into the hot oil. Prepare the tempura in several batches. Let the pieces fry for 5 to 6 minutes, or until they're golden brown, then drain them on paper towels.

7 Serve with the chocolate sauce transferred to a dipping bowl or spooned over the top.

HINT
For a slightly lighter version, you can opt to sprinkle the tempura pieces with confectioner's sugar and a few drops of lemon juice just before serving instead of the melted chocolate.

Japanese Cheesecake

You probably know the traditional New York version, but souffle-style Japanese cheese-cake is quite different—crustless, less sweet and baked to become much spongier and lighter. Give it a try; you might find you like it even better than regular cheesecake!

PREPARATION: 25 minutes
COOKING TIME: 1 hour 10 minutes
RESTING TIME: 3 hours

SERVES 10

1¼ cups (280 g) cream cheese
5 eggs
⅔ cup (120 g) superfine sugar
¼ cup (50 ml) milk
1½ tablespoons (20 g) butter
½ lemon, juiced and zested
½ cup (60 g) flour
2 tablespoons (20 g) cornstarch
A pinch of salt

For serving (optional)
Strawberries or mixed berries

1 Make sure all your ingredients are at room temperature and preheat the oven to 355°F (180°C).
2 Cut a circle of parchment paper, using it to line a deep 8-inch (20-cm) cake pan.
3 In a mixing bowl, whip the cream cheese until it's texture. Separate the eggs. Incorporate the yolks, one at a time, into the cream cheese. Add half of the sugar, mixing it in quickly.
4 In a saucepan, heat the milk and butter until the butter melts. Pour it on top of the cream cheese mix-ture and whip. Add the lemon juice and zest and mix. Sift the flour, cornstarch and salt, adding it to the bowl. Mix well.
5 Whip the egg whites at low speed, adding half of the remaining sugar. Increase the speed and add the remaining sugar, beating all the while. Stop when the whites are firm.

Japanese Cheesecake (continued)

6 Incorporate the beaten egg whites in three stages. Pour the batter into the cake pan.

7 Set it in a hot water bath and bake it for 15 minutes. Lower the oven temperature to 300°F (150°C) and continue baking for 55 minutes.

8 Turn off the oven, but let the cheesecake remain in the oven for 30 minutes. Then remove it and chill it in the fridge for at least 2 hours.

9 Unmold the cheesecake and serve it with seasonal fruit and whipped cream.

You can always prepare your cheesecake the day before. The extra day in the fridge makes it even better!

Black Sesame Panna Cotta

A fusion favorite, this smooth, cool and delicate dessert is elevated by the nutty fragrance and flavor of black sesame. Some like a red fruit coulis on top, made of cherries and strawberries, while others prefer it unadorned.

PREPARATION: 10 minutes
COOKING TIME: 3 minutes
RESTING TIME: 1 hour

MAKES 4 SMALL JARS

6½ tablespoons (60 g) black
    sesame seeds
3 tablespoons sesame paste
¾ cup (200 ml) heavy cream
1 cup (250 ml) milk
⅓ cup (65 g) superfine sugar
½ teaspoon agar-agar powder

1 Crush the sesame seeds in a mortar.
2 Place the sesame paste in a mixing bowl and slowly add the cream, stirring all the while until it's smooth.
3 In a saucepan, mix the milk, sugar and agar-agar.
4 Heat the mixture on medium, stirring constantly. Bring to a boil for 15 seconds. Add the cream-sesame paste mixture and the crushed sesame seeds. Mix well, then divide into four serving jars or bowls. Let them set in the fridge for at least one hour before serving.

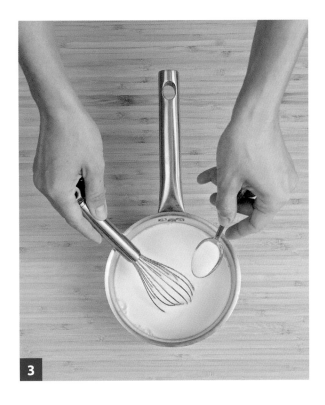

Chocolate Tofu Mousse

The whipped consistency of silky tofu is what sets this mousse apart. Like Japanese cheesecake, it's lighter and not as sweet as dairy-based versions, while still retaining the smooth and luscious texture of a homemade pudding.

PREPARATION: 5 minutes
COOKING TIME: 5 minutes
RESTING TIME: 5 hours

SERVES 4

10 oz (300 g) silky tofu
6 oz (180 g) dark baking chocolate or 1 cup chips
3 tablespoons agave or maple syrup
3 tablespoons kinako (toasted soybean flour)
Fresh berries or currents (optional, to garnish)

1 Drain the tofu in a colander for 10 minutes. Melt the chocolate in a double-boiler.

2 Remove the chocolate from the heat and add the agave syrup, half of the kinako and the drained tofu. Mix with an immersion blender for a few minutes.

3 Divide the mousse into four ramekins.

4 Chill in the fridge for at least 5 hours. Remove from the fridge an hour before serving. Sprinkle with the remaining kinako and serve topped with berries or currents, if you wish.

Black Sesame Eclairs

Black sesame seeds are nothing new in the pastry world. Bakers have turned to them for their earthy, nutty and distinctive flavor for years. Here a French favorite is given a hint of Japanese flair for a uniquely elegant confection.

PREPARATION: 35 minutes
COOKING TIME: 30 minutes
RESTING TIME: 15 minutes

MAKES 16 ECLAIRS

For the Sesame Cream
4 egg yolks
⅓ cup (70 g) superfine sugar
4 tablespoons (35 g) cornstarch
1½ cups (350 ml) whole milk
2 tablespoons (20 g) crushed sesame seeds
3 tablespoons (45 g) sesame paste

For the Chou Dough
3½ tablespoons (50 g) butter
½ cup (70 g) flour
½ cup (125 ml) water
1 teaspoon superfine sugar
A dash of salt
2 large eggs

Prepare the Sesame Cream
1 In a bowl, blend the egg yolks with the sugar and cornstarch.
2 Bring the milk to a boil in a saucepan. Pour it into the egg mixture, stirring quickly. Pour the mixture back into the pan, add the crushed sesame seeds and heat on low while whisking constantly. As soon as the mixture thickens, remove it from heat and add the sesame paste.
3 Cover it with plastic wrap pressed tight onto the surface. Let it cool to room temperature, then chill it in the fridge.

Prepare the Chou Pastry
4 Preheat the oven to 355°F (180°C). Dice the butter into small cubes. Sift the flour. Pour the water into a pan and add the butter, sugar and salt.
5 Heat on low, removing it as soon as it starts to boil. Add the sifted flour, stirring until it's evenly mixed. Put the pan back on low heat and whisk until the dough peels away easily from the edges of the pan. Add the eggs one at a time and whisk after the addition of each. Place the dough in a piping bag.
6 Using the piping bag, make 15 thin logs about 5 inches (12.5 cm) long on a baking sheet lined with parchment paper.

Black Sesame Eclairs (continued)

For the Glaze
3½ oz (100 g) white fondant icing
1 tablespoon water
2 tablespoons black sesame seeds

7 Bake for 25 minutes. Turn off the heat, letting the éclairs remain in the oven for 15 minutes more.

8 Once they've cooled, cut the éclairs lengthwise using a serrated knife.

9 Remove the cream from the fridge. Whip it then add it to a piping bag and fill the éclairs.

Finish with the Glaze

10 In a pan, heat the fondant with the water and sesame seeds on low, stirring until smooth. Dip each eclair into the glaze to add a rich smear on top.

11 Spoon a bit more of the glaze on top, if you like.

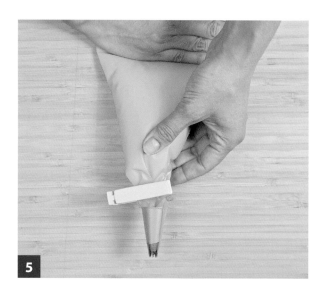

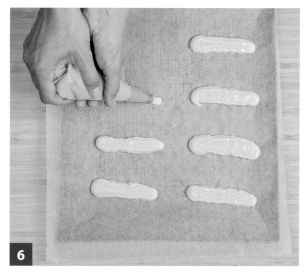

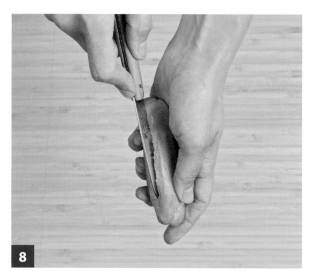

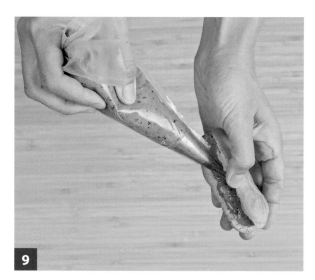

Black Sesame Madeleines

Black sesame seeds appear throughout the dessert world—in tuiles, ice creams, cakes, doughnuts, chocolate bars and truffles. But one of my favorite combinations is to add them to the simple pleasure of the madeleine. Are they cakes or cookies? Have one more before you make up your mind! (Bamboo charcoal powder is a popular food coloring in Asia and is available in Asian grocery stores. It has no flavor and can be omitted, if you wish.)

PREPARATION: 10 minutes
COOKING TIME: 10 minutes
RESTING TIME: 10 minutes

MAKES 16

2 eggs
½ cup (100 g) superfine sugar
5 tablespoons (70 g) butter
4½ tablespoons (70 g) black sesame paste
1 heaping cup (140 g) flour
1 tablespoon bamboo charcoal powder
 (optional)
3 tablespoons black sesame seeds
½ teaspoon baking powder

1 Preheat the oven to 425°F (220°C).
2 In a mixing bowl, whisk the eggs and sugar until the mixture is foamy. Melt the butter, then add in the black sesame paste. Pour it into the egg mixture and whisk.
3 Crush the black sesame seeds in a mortar. In a bowl, mix the flour, bamboo charcoal powder (if you're using it), crushed sesame seeds and baking powder.
4 Incorporate this into the egg mixture. Let it rest for 10 minutes, then pour it into greased madeleine molds so it fills ¾ of each. Bake for about 8 minutes. then unmold and cool them on a rack.

Matcha Desserts

Matcha, the soothing beverage and centerpiece of the celebrated tea ceremony, has now moved beyond the teapot, expanding its repertoire to become an ingredient featured in a range of sweet and savory recipes.

Its distinctive texture allows it to blend easily with desserts. Appearing in a variety of sweetened guises (including cakes, quickbreads, tiramisus, shortbread, ice cream and macarons), its light green color draws the eye while its subtle taste brings an often bitter or earthy counterpoint to the sweetness of the dessert.

Matcha is a new and unexpected dessert star. Does it matter that it's also healthy? Maybe for some!

Matcha Tiramisu

The vibrant green color of this decadent dessert isn't the only indication that it's a modern Japanese twist on a classic Italian favorite. Rich and creamy, the layers of green-tea-soaked biscuits contrast with the light and airy mascarpone cream.

PREPARATION: 15 minutes
COOKING TIME: 2 hours

SERVES 4

2 eggs, separated
⅓ cup (60 g) superfine sugar
1 cup (200 g) mascarpone
A pinch of salt
1 tablespoon matcha powder
½ cup (120 ml) hot water
8 ladyfinger cookies

1 Prepare the mascarpone cream: In a mixing bowl, whisk the egg yolks with the sugar, then add the mascarpone, mixing until smooth.

2 Whisk the egg whites, with a dash of salt, until stiff peaks form, then gently fold them into the yolk mixture. Infuse half of the matcha in the water.

3 Dip the cookies in the tea, then line half of them along the bottom of a deep dish.

4 Layer half the cream onto the cookies. Add a layer of the remaining cookies and end with a final layer of the mascarpone cream.

5 Chill the tiramisu in the fridge for at least 2 hours or, ideally, overnight. Using a fine-mesh sieve, sprinkle the rest of the matcha on top before serving.

Strawberry Matcha Layer Cake

For a memorable birthday cake or an anytime craving, this scrumptious creation combines soft, fluffy matcha sponge cake with layers of fruit and mascarpone cream. The sweet-tart strawberries pair perfectly with the earthy green tea. It's a "matcha" made in heaven!

PREPARATION: 45 minutes
COOKING TIME: 40 minutes
RESTING TIME: 2 hours

SERVES 8 TO 10 (8-IN OR 20-CM CAKE PAN)

5 eggs
½ cup (100 g) **superfine sugar**
⅓ cup (80 ml) **sunflower oil**
¼ cup (50 ml) **milk**
¾ cup (100 g) **flour**
1 teaspoon **baking powder**
1 tablespoon **matcha powder**

For the Cream
½ cup (120 g) **mascarpone**
1 cup (250 ml) **whipping cream**
½ cup (60 g) **confectioner's sugar**

1 Separate the eggs. Preheat the oven to 355°F (180°C).
2 Cut a circle of parchment paper to line the bottom of a deep 8-inch (20-cm) cake pan.
3 In a mixing bowl, whisk the egg yolks with half of the sugar until foamy. Add the oil, whisk again, then pour in the milk and blend.
4 In another bowl, sift the flour, baking powder and matcha. Add the dry ingredients to the egg mixture.

Prepare the Cream
5 Whip the egg whites on low speed. When they form stiff peaks, add half of the remaining sugar. Increase the speed and add the remaining sugar, whipping all the while. When the egg whites are firm, fold them into the batter, then pour it into the cake pan.
6 Bake for 40 minutes. Check the doneness with a toothpick or the tip of a knife. When it comes out clean, remove the cake and cool it on a rack.
7 Whip the mascarpone, cream and sugar until stiff peaks form. Place it in a piping bag and chill it in the fridge.

Strawberry Matcha Layer Cake
(continued)

For the Garnish
½ lb (250 g) strawberries
Matcha powder, to sprinkle on top

8 Hull the strawberries, reserving two or three for the garnish. Dice a third of the berries and cut the remaining ones in half.

9 Unmold the cooled cake and slice it into two equal layers with a serrated knife.

10 Set one disk into a cake ring. Arrange the halved strawberries along the outer edge. Add half the cream to the center of the ring of halved berries, covering with the diced berries.

11 Set the second cake disk on top.

12 Then spread the remaining cream on top.

13 Chill in the fridge for at least 1 hour. Before serving, sprinkle the cake with matcha and garnish it with the reserved strawberries.

Matcha Hazelnut Butter-Yogurt Cake

Yogurt is the secret to the light texture of this luscious matcha quickbread. The ubiquitous black sesame seeds make another appearance here, further elevating this simplest of teatime treats.

PREPARATION: 20 minutes
COOKING TIME: 40 minutes
RESTING TIME: 30 minutes

SERVES 10

A rectangular pan (8 in/20 cm long)
⅔ cup (100 g) hazelnuts
7 tablespoons (100 g) butter
½ cup (120 g) plain yogurt
2 eggs
¾ cup (150 g) superfine sugar
1¼ cups (150 g) flour
1 teaspoon baking powder
1 tablespoon matcha powder
1 tablespoon black sesame seeds

1 Toast the hazelnuts in a pan set on medium heat. Shake the pan occasionally so the nuts don't burn or overtoast. When they start to turn brown, toast them an additional 2 minutes. Then finely grind them.

2 Preheat the oven to 350°F (180°C). Melt the butter. In a mixing bowl, whisk the yogurt with the eggs and the sugar. Add the melted butter. In a second mixing bowl, sift the flour with the baking powder and the matcha.

3 Blend the wet and dry ingredients together.

4 Add the hazelnuts. Line a cake pan with parchment paper and pour in the batter. Sprinkle the black sesame seeds on top.

5 Bake for 45 minutes. Check the doneness with a toothpick or the tip of a knife inserted in the middle. When it comes out clean, remove and cool the cake on a baking rack before serving.

Matcha Raspberry Macarons

A Franco-Japanese concoction, a plate full of these tasty macarons disappears as soon as I set them out for guests. One is not enough, the tangy raspberry cradled between the crunchy green shells. The slight bitterness of the matcha provides the perfect balance.

PREPARATION: 50 minutes
COOKING TIME: 25 minutes
RESTING TIME: 1 hour

MAKES 24 MACARONS

For the Raspberry Coulis
1¼ cups (150 g) fresh or frozen raspberries
⅓ cup (80 g) superfine sugar

For the Matcha Shells
1 cup (100 g) ground roasted almonds
¾ cup (100 g) confectioner's sugar
2 large egg whites, at room temperature
½ cup (100 g) superfine sugar
2 tablespoons matcha powder
2 tablespoons water

Prepare the Raspberry Coulis

1 In a small heavy-bottomed pan, cook the raspberries and sugar on low heat, stirring occasionally, for about 4 minutes. Using a hand mixer, blend the mixture to create a smooth coulis.

2 Cook for 4 more minutes to thicken the coulis. Remove from the heat and cool to room temperature before chilling it in the fridge.

Prepare the Matcha Shells

3 Mix the almond meal and the confectioner's sugar. Sift them into a mixing bowl.

4 Add the sugar to a pan, then add the matcha and water, blending with a spatula.

5 Heat on medium and check the temperature with a thermometer.

6 When the matcha syrup reaches 210°F (100°C), start whipping the egg whites.

7 Pour half of the egg whites into the bowl of an electric mixer. When the whites are almost firm and the syrup has reached 245°F (118°C), pour it on top of the egg whites, beating continuously until the meringue is firm.

8 Combine the rest of the whipped egg whites with the dry ingredients. Incorporate the matcha meringue into the almond mixture a little at a time. Fold it in with a spatula until the batter is smooth.

Matcha Raspberry Macarons
(continued)

For the Garnish
24 small fresh raspberries

HINT
In order to prevent the macarons from cracking, open the oven door briefly a few times while baking them.

9 Preheat the oven to 300°F (150°C).

10 Using a piping bag, make 1.5-inch (3.8-cm) disks on a baking sheet lined with parchment paper. You should get 48 disks for two sheets. Bake the macarons 12 to 14 minutes. Let them cool for 5 minutes before removing them from the sheets.

11 To assemble the macarons, cut the cooled shells in half. Slather one half with raspberry coulis. Place a fresh raspberry in the middle of the coulis, then add the top half of the shell.

12 Let the macarons sit in the fridge for at least an hour before serving.

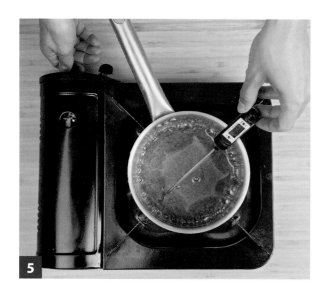

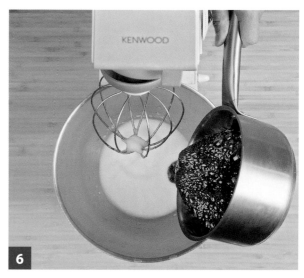

Matcha Butter Almond Cookies

The richness of butter cookies is brought down to earth with a healthy shot of matcha. You can leave out the almonds or if you're a true nut lover, try roasted pecans instead.

PREPARATION: 20 minutes
COOKING TIME: 30 minutes
RESTING TIME: 12 minutes

MAKES 20

1¼ cups (150 g) flour
6 tablespoons (80 g) superfine sugar
⅓ cup (40 g) ground roasted almonds (see page 106)
2 tablespoons matcha powder
A pinch of salt
5 tablespoons (70 g) diced butter, at room temperature
1 egg

1 In the bowl of a mixer, combine the flour, sugar, almond meal, matcha and salt. Add the diced butter. Mix on medium speed to form a loose consistency, then fold in the egg. Mix until a firm ball of dough forms. If needed, adjust with a little flour or water.
2 Form the dough into a log and wrap it in plastic wrap. Chill it in the fridge for at least 30 minutes.
3 Preheat the oven to 350°F (180°C). Remove the plastic wrap and slice the log into 20 disks. Set them on a baking sheet lined with parchment paper. Bake for 10 to 12 minutes, depending on the degree of doneness you prefer.

HINT
Roast the almonds before grinding them to intensify the flavor. If you have almond meal on hand, of course use that instead!

Lemon Matcha Tartlets

Talk about a perfect pairing! Citrus and matcha are made for each other, and the proof is in these tartlets. Matcha shortbread filled with a custardy lemon cream. Add the meringue to make the perfect decadent dessert!

PREPARATION: 45 minutes
COOKING TIME: 1 hour
RESTING TIME: 16 to 18 minutes

MAKES ONE 10-IN (26-CM) PIE OR 10 TARTLETS

For the Matcha Shortbread Dough
4¼ tablespoons (60 g) butter, at room temperature
1 cup (125 g) whole-grain flour
¼ cup (50 g) superfine sugar
1 tablespoon matcha
A pinch of salt
1 egg yolk

Prepare the Matcha Shortbread Dough

1 Preheat the oven to 350°F (180°C).

2 Dice the butter into small cubes. In the bowl of a mixer, blend the flour, sugar, matcha and salt. Add the diced butter. Mix on medium speed to create a loose consistency, then add the egg yolk.

3 Mix until a firm ball of dough forms, adjusting it, if necessary, with a little flour or water.

4 Roll out the dough, using a rolling pin or your hands, to fit the pie or tart pans you're using. Prick the dough with a fork, then bake for 8 to 10 minutes or until golden brown.

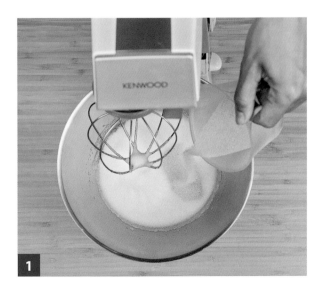

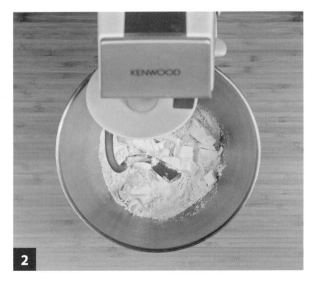

Lemon Matcha Tartlets (continued)

For the Lemon Cream Filling
2 lemons, juiced
3 eggs
6½ tablespoons (80 g) superfine sugar
1 tablespoon cornstarch

For the Matcha Meringue
½ cup (60 g) confectioner's sugar
1 tablespoon matcha powder
¼ teaspoon baking powder
2 egg whites

Prepare the Lemon Cream Filling
5 In a saucepan, combine the lemon juice, sugar, eggs and cornstarch, whisking until foamy.
6 Heat the mixture on low, stirring with a spatula until it starts to thicken.
7 Spread the cream onto the cooled pie crust or the tartlet crusts.

Prepare the Matcha Meringue
8 In a mixing bowl, combine the sugar, matcha and baking powder. Using an electric beater on low speed, whisk the egg whites until they're opaque. Fold half of the dry ingredients into the bowl. Then add the rest, stirring constantly.
9 Using a piping bag, garnish the pie or tartlets with meringue rosettes. Bake the meringue in the oven or use a cooking torch.
10 Chill the pie or tartlets at least 1 hour before serving. You can make the pie or tartlets the day before, just add the meringue right before serving.

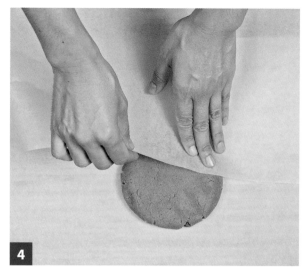

Matcha Almond Chocolate Truffles

Kids love these two-bite treats, especially when the green filling is revealed. Adult chocolate fiends will adore the novelty. Once you see how easy it is to assemble and dip these delicacies, you'll wish you'd made a double batch.

PREPARATION: 25 minutes
COOKING TIME: 5 minutes
FREEZING TIME: 30 minutes
RESTING TIME: 2 hours 40 minutes

MAKES 20

1¼ cups (7 oz/200 g) white chocolate
¼ cup (30 g) almond meal
A pinch of salt
1 tablespoon matcha powder
⅓ cup plus 1 tablespoon (100 ml) whipping cream
1½ tablespoons (20 g) butter, at room temperature
¼ cup (2½ oz/70 g) dark chocolate squares

1 Prepare the matcha ganache filling. In a mixing bowl, break the white chocolate into pieces. Add the almond meal, salt and matcha. Heat the cream in a saucepan. As soon as it starts to boil, add it to the mixing bowl. Stir and blend until the chocolate is melted. Dice the butter and add it to the mixture, blending well. Cover it with plastic wrap and chill for 2 hours.
2 Form the matcha ganache into 20 balls and place them in the freezer for 30 minutes until they harden.
3 Melt the dark chocolate in a double-boiler. Using a long-pronged fork, dip the balls in the melted chocolate until covered, then set them on parchment paper. Let the truffles cool until the shells have hardened.

Matcha Chocolate-Filled Cupcakes

Move over, red velvet! These hazelnut-infused matcha morsels are tasty enough. To find a gooey chocolate filling inside puts this uncommon cupcake over the top.

PREPARATION: 15 minutes
COOKING TIME: 8 minutes

MAKES 6

3 eggs
½ cup (100 g) superfine sugar
4 teaspoons (8 g) matcha powder
2 tablespoons hot water
7 tablespoons (100 g) butter
1 cup (120 g) flour
4 tablespoons (30 g) cornstarch
A pinch of salt
⅔ cup (70 g) ground roasted hazelnuts (see page 106)
2 cups (12 oz/335 g) dark chocolate squares

1 Preheat the oven to 350°F (180°C). In a mixing bowl, whip the eggs with the sugar until the mix is foamy. Dilute the matcha in the hot water. Melt the butter. Add the matcha and melted butter to the mixing bowl.
2 In another mixing bowl, combine the flour, cornstarch, salt and ground hazelnuts. Mix the contents of the two bowls together.
3 Grease the muffin pan or use individual paper muffin cups. Pour the batter in the cups, filling each halfway. Place 2 chocolate squares (or a sixth of the total chocolate) in the middle of each. Add the rest of the batter to cover the chocolate and bake for 8 minutes. Allow them to cool for a few minutes, but serve them right away while the chocolate is still melted.

Other Asian Desserts

Now it's time for a pan-Asian dessert tour! You'll notice the influences that crop up and the cultural borrowing that occurs when certain desserts go global.

Korean Cinnamon Walnut Pancakes are light and satisfying and can play a starring role at any weekend brunch. Tapioca is elevated to create a Thai classic, and we'll also tap into the amazing flavors and rich tradition of the Chinese bakery with some hot-out-of-the-oven treats. What could be better?

Coconut Passionfruit Tapioca Pearls

If you love coconut as much as I do, this recipe will become a regular in your dessert repertoire. The passionfruit-mango topping gives way to the creamy texture of tapioca pearls below.

PREPARATION: 10 minutes
COOKING TIME: 20 minutes
RESTING TIME: 2 hours

SERVES 4

4 tablespoons dried tapioca pearls
2½ cups (600 ml) coconut milk
¼ teaspoon vanilla extract
2½ tablespoons superfine sugar

For the Topping
½ mango
1 passionfruit
Zest of 1 lime

1 Set the tapioca pearls in a saucepan with half of the coconut milk. Let it rest for an hour, then add the remaining coconut milk, vanilla and sugar. Bring to a boil and simmer for 15 to 20 minutes on low, stirring regularly until it reaches a pudding-like consistency.
2 Divide the mixture into 4 glass jars or cups. Chill in the fridge for at least an hour.
3 Before serving, peel and dice the half mango. Scoop the pulp from the passionfruit. Garnish the tapioca creams with the fruit and sprinkle the lime zest on top.

Hong Kong Egg Tartlets

A common sight in Chinese bakeries and dim sum restaurants, these tarts resemble tiny pies. Filled with a smooth, lightly sweetened egg custard, they're at their best when fresh out of the oven.

PREPARATION: 10 minutes
COOKING TIME: 20 minutes
RESTING TIME: 2 hours

MAKES 30 TARTLETS

For the Butter Dough
1½ cups (200 g) flour
1 egg, beaten
1¼ sticks (10 tablespoons/140 g) butter, at room temperature
1 tablespoon superfine sugar
A pinch of salt

For the Plain Dough
1 egg yolk
1½ cups (200 g) flour
⅓ cup (80 ml) water
A pinch salt

Prepare the Butter Dough

1 In a mixing bowl, combine the flour, sugar and salt. Dice the butter. Add the cubes to the flour using a wooden spoon. Then add the beaten egg, mixing thoroughly to form a ball.

2 Wrap the dough in plastic wrap and chill it in the fridge for at least 20 minutes.

Prepare the Plain Dough

3 Combine the ingredients in a food processor. Mix until a firm ball of dough forms.

4 Remove the plastic wrap from the Butter Dough. Using a rolling pin, roll out each ball of dough separately, to about a ¼ inch thick, then place the Butter Dough layer on top of the Plain Dough.

5 Follow the photos to combine the two layers. If it's easier, use a sheet of plastic wrap when combining the layers.

6 Wrap it in plastic wrap and chill it in the fridge for 30 minutes.

Hong Kong Egg Tartlets (continued)

For the Egg Cream
1 cup (250 ml) milk
½ cup (100 g) superfine sugar
A few drops vanilla extract
3 eggs

Prepare the Egg Cream

7 Preheat oven to 390°F (200°C). Combine the milk, vanilla extract and sugar in a saucepan. Heat on low until the sugar is dissolved. In a mixing bowl, beat the eggs. Add them to the hot milk mixture, stirring constantly. Strain the cream through a fine-mesh sieve.

Assemble and Bake the Tartlets

8 Remove the dough from the fridge. Cut 4-inch (10-cm) circles using a biscuit cutter.

9 Set the doug circles in a buttered tartlet pan containing 3-inch (8-cm) cups. Divide the egg cream among the tartlets, spooning it on top of the dough.

10 Bake the tartlets for 20 minutes. After 10 minutes, lower the temperature to 320°F (160°C). Enjoy the tartlets warm.

For a quicker version, you can use storebought phyllo dough instead of the shortbread/water dough mix.

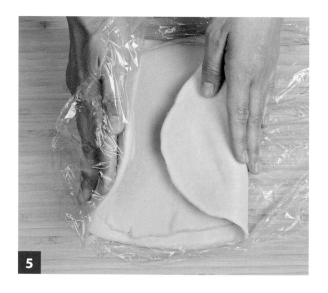

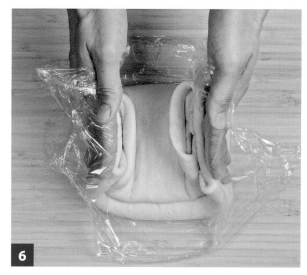

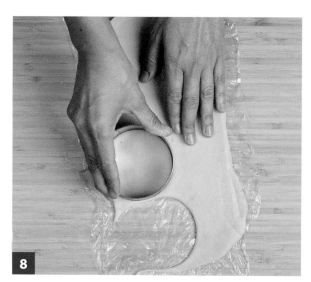

Sesame Tuile Cookies

A blend of golden and black sesame seeds really sets these delicate cookies apart. This is another good recipe to double, as once you set out a stack of these, the pile disappears very quickly!

PREPARATION: 10 minutes
COOKING TIME: 10 minutes
RESTING TIME: 15 minutes

MAKES 12

1 large egg white
3 tablespoons (40 g) **superfine sugar**
A pinch of **salt**
⅓ cup (40 g) **flour**
1½ tablespoons (20 g) **butter**
½ cup (80 g) **golden and black sesame seeds**

HINT
These cookies keep well in a sealed container. Make sure they're completely cooled first, to retain their signature crunch.

1 Preheat the oven to 320°F (160°C).

2 In a mixing bowl, blend the egg white, sugar and salt until foamy. Melt the butter and add it to the bowl along with the sifted flour. Mix well, then fold in the sesame seeds.

3 Place a tablespoon of the dough on a baking sheet lined with parchment paper. Flatten it with a fork to create a disk that's about 3 inches (8 cm) wide.

4 Bake for 8 to 10 minutes. Remove from the oven and place the cookies on a baking rack. Let cool before serving.

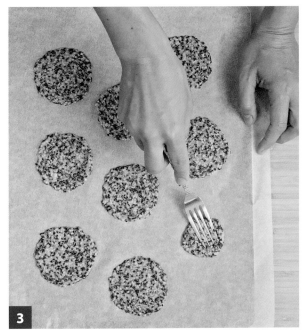

Sweet Coconut Buns

Chewy and loaded with coconut, these nuomici, as the Chinese call them, pair a soft and sweet mung bean puree with a traditional rice-flour casing. Let them cool before serving to be sure they take shape and solidify.

PREPARATION: 30 minutes
COOKING TIME: 35 minutes
RESTING TIME: 1 hour 15 minutes

MAKES 10

For the Filling
¾ cup (5 oz/150 g) shelled yellow
   mung beans
⅓ cup plus 1 tablespoon (80 g)
   superfine sugar
A pinch of salt
¾ cup (60 g) shredded coconut

Prepare the Filling

1 Soak the mung beans in hot water for an hour. Rinse drain them well, then cook them in three times their volume of water for 25 minutes or until they're soft.

2 Skim off the foam after 12 minutes. At the end of the 25 minutes, drain the beans and let them cool for 15 minutes.

3 In a saucepan, mix the cooked beans with the sugar, salt and ⅓ of the shredded coconut. Reserve the remaining coconut for coating the outside of the buns.

4 Cook the mixture on low for 5 minutes, stirring constantly with a spatula to create a dry, pasty consistency. Let it cool, then form the filling into 10 small balls.

Sweet Coconut Buns (continued)

For the Dough

2 cups (240 g) sticky rice flour

¾ cup plus 1 tablespoon (200 ml) water

4 heaping tablespoons (60 g) superfine sugar

A pinch of salt

Prepare the Dough

5 In a mixing bowl, combine all the dough ingredients.

6 Divide the dough into ten balls, flattening each in your palm to form a 2-in (5-cm) disk. On each disk, place a ball of the filling.

7 Wrap the dough around it, completely enclosing it.

8 In a large pan, bring water to a boil. Drop the balls in, one after another, working in several batches. Let them cook for a few minutes.

9 When they rise to the surface, let them cook for an additional 2 minutes, then remove them from the pot.

10 Drain the balls and roll them in the reserved shredded coconut. Enjoy them warm. To preserve their softness and texture, wrap the leftovers individually in plastic wrap. Keep them for at most 2 days at room temperature.

Korean Cinnamon Walnut Pancakes

You may be familiar with the savory kind, but a sweet Korean pancake? Here, an irresistible blend of walnuts, cinnamon and brown sugar is stuffed inside a tasty griddle cake. Perfect for breakfast, brunch or any time of day.

PREPARATION: 25 minutes
COOKING TIME: 15 minutes
RESTING TIME: 1 hour

MAKES 8

For the Pancakes
1¼ cups (150 g) white flour
⅔ cup (80 g) sticky rice flour
1 tablespoon superfine sugar
2½ teaspoons quick-rising yeast
1 teaspoon salt
¾ cup plus 1 tablespoon (200 ml) milk
1 tablespoon olive oil
Vegetable oil, to grease the pan

For the Stuffing
3 tablespoons walnuts
1 teaspoon cinnamon
4 tablespoons brown sugar

Prepare the Pancakes

1 In a mixing bowl, combine the two flours, sugar, yeast and salt.

2 Combine the milk and olive oil. Add it to the dry ingredients, blending until smooth. Cover the bowl with a clean towel and let the dough rise for 1 hour at room temperature. When the dough has doubled in volume, punch or press it back down, then let it rest for a few minutes.

3 Meanwhile, prepare the stuffing by blending all the ingredients in a mixer or a food processor.

4 Take an eighth of the dough and flatten it out in your palm. Set 1 tablespoon of stuffing in the middle, then enclose the stuffing with the dough, forming a ball.

5 Repeat until you have eight balls. Heat a little vegetable oil in a frying pan and set two or three balls on the bottom, depending on the pan's size.

6 Flatten them with a spatula to a thickness of about ⅓ inch (1 cm). Cook for 2 to 3 minutes, then flip and cook for an additional 2 minutes. Drain them on a paper towel. Repeat with the remaining pancakes and enjoy them warm.

Sweet Black Sesame Balls

A honeyed black-sesame paste awaits, cradled inside these crispy fried bread balls. Called jian dui, this chewy treat is traditionally made with glutinous rice flour and coated with an extra layer of sesame seeds, a double dose of sesame flavor!

PREPARATION: 20 minutes
COOKING TIME: 15 minutes

MAKES 12

For the Stuffing
3½ tablespoons (50 g) black sesame paste
3½ tablespoons (30 g) black sesame seeds
2 tablespoons (45 g) honey
A pinch of salt

For the Dough
1 cup (120 g) sticky rice flour
¼ cup (50 g) superfine sugar
⅓ cup (80 ml) water
3 tablespoons white sesame seeds

Vegetable oil, for frying

1 In a bowl, combine the stuffing ingredients, then chill the mixture in the fridge.
2 In a mixing bowl, combine the sticky rice flour, sugar and water. Form the dough into twelve balls.
3 Place a ball in your palm and flatten it to create a disk. Place 1 tablespoon of stuffing in the middle and enclose it with the dough. Roll the ball in the sesame seeds, then set it aside. Repeat with the remaining dough.
4 Heat the vegetable oil in a wide-bottomed pan. Fry the sesame balls in several batches, flipping them after 2 minutes. When they're golden brown, remove them from the oil and drain them on paper towels. Enjoy warm.

Strawberry Wontons

If tempura can be made into a dessert, why not wontons? A fruit-filled fusion of sweet strawberry and crispy dough, it's a jelly doughnut in disguise. The mung bean-coconut filling is what pulls it all together.

PREPARATION: 15 minutes
COOKING TIME: 30 minutes

MAKES 20

20 hulled strawberries
20 egg wonton wrappers (3.5 in/ 9 cm in diameter)
Vegetable oil, for frying

For the Filling
⅔ cup (4 oz/120 g) shelled yellow mung beans
½ cup (40 g) shredded coconut
⅓ cup (60 g) superfine sugar
A pinch of salt

1 Prepare the Filling by following the recipe on page 132.
2 Add 1 teaspoon of the Filling to the center of a wonton wrapper. Garnish it with a strawberry.
3 Wet the four edges of the wrapper and seal the wonton by joining the corners in the center, just above the strawberry. Refer to the photos below.
4 Heat the oil in a deep pan. Fry the wontons in batches, letting them cook for a few minutes, then flip them over and cook for a minute or two more.
5 When they're crisp and golden brown, remove them from the oil and drain them on paper towels. Enjoy them warm.

Measurements

Metric	Imperial equivalent	Volume
5 ml	1 teaspoon	
15 ml	1 tablespoon	
30 ml	⅛ cup	1 oz
60 ml	¼ cup	2 oz
120 ml	½ cup	4 oz
240 ml	1 cup	8 oz
480 ml	2 cups or 1 pint	
1 liter	4⅛ cups	

Metric	Imperial equivalent	Weight
30 g	¹⁄₁₆ lb	1 oz
55 g	⅛ lb	2 oz
115 g	¼ lb	4 oz
170 g	⅜ lb	6 oz
225 g	½ lb	8 oz
454 g	1 pound	16 oz

Heat	Celsius		Fahrenheit
Very low	70°C		160°F
Low	100°C		210°F
Low	120°C		250°F
Medium	150°C		300°F
Medium	180°C		350°F
High	200°C		390°F
High	230°C		450°F
Very High	260°C		500°F

"Books to Span the East and West"

Tuttle Publishing was founded in 1832 in the small New England town of Rutland, Vermont (USA). Our core values remain as strong today as they were then—to publish best-in-class books which bring people together one page at a time. In 1948, we established a publishing outpost in Japan—and Tuttle is now a leader in publishing English-language books about the arts, languages and cultures of Asia. The world has become a much smaller place today and Asia's economic and cultural influence has grown. Yet the need for meaningful dialogue and information about this diverse region has never been greater. Over the past seven decades, Tuttle has published thousands of books on subjects ranging from martial arts and paper crafts to language learning and literature—and our talented authors, illustrators, designers and photographers have won many prestigious awards. We welcome you to explore the wealth of information available on Asia at www.tuttlepublishing.com.

Published by Tuttle Publishing, an imprint of Periplus Editions (HK) Ltd.

www.tuttlepublishing.com

Patisseries Japonaises, originally published by Mango Editions.

English translation © 2023 Periplus Editions.

Photographs by Patrice Hauser
Translation by Marie S. Velde

ISBN 978-4-8053-1770-9

26 25 24 23   10 9 8 7 6 5 4 3 2 1
Printed in China   2307EP

Distributed by

North America, Latin America & Europe
Tuttle Publishing
364 Innovation Drive
North Clarendon, VT 05759-9436 U.S.A.
Tel: 1 (802) 773-8930 | Fax: 1 (802) 773-6993
info@tuttlepublishing.com
www.tuttlepublishing.com

Japan
Tuttle Publishing
Yaekari Building 3rd Floor
5-4-12 Osaki
Shinagawa-ku
Tokyo 141-0032
Tel: (81) 3 5437-0171 | Fax: (81) 3 5437-0755
sales@tuttle.co.jp
www.tuttle.co.jp

Asia Pacific
Berkeley Books Pte. Ltd.
3 Kallang Sector #04-01
Singapore 349278
Tel: (65) 6741 2178 | Fax: (65) 6741 2179
inquiries@periplus.com.sg
www.tuttlepublishing.com